COSTUME AROUND THE WORLD
Saudi Arabia

Cath Senker

CHELSEA CLUB HOUSE

An Imprint of Chelsea House Publishers

Produced for Chelsea Clubhouse by Bailey Publishing Associates Ltd
11a Woodlands, Hove BN3 6TJ
England

Project Manager: Roberta Bailey
Editor: Alex Woolf
Text Designer: Jane Hawkins
Picture Research: Roberta Bailey and Shelley Noronha

Chelsea Clubhouse
An imprint of Chelsea House Publishers
132 West 31st Street
New York NY 10001

ISBN 978-0-7910-9773-1

Library of Congress Cataloging-in-Publication Data
Costume around the world.—1st ed.
      v. cm.
      Includes bibliographical references and index.
      Contents: [1] China / Anne Rooney—[2] France / Kathy Elgin—[3] Germany / Cath Senker—[4] India / Kathy Elgin—[5] Italy / Kathy Elgin—[6] Japan / Jane Bingham—[7] Mexico / Jane Bingham—[8] Saudi Arabia / Cath Senker—[9] Spain / Kathy Elgin—[10] United States / Liz Gogerly.
      ISBN 978-0-7910-9765-6 (v. 1)—ISBN 978-0-7910-9766-3 (v. 2)—ISBN 978-0-7910-9767-0 (v. 3)—ISBN 978-0-7910-9768-7 (v. 4)—ISBN 978-0-7910-9769-4 (v. 5)—ISBN 978-0-7910-9770-0 (v. 6)—ISBN 978-0-7910-9771-7 (v. 7)—ISBN 978-0-7910-9773-1 (v. 8)— ISBN 978-0-7910-9772-4 (v. 9)—ISBN 978-0-7910-9774-8 (v. 10) 1. Clothing and dress—Juvenile literature.
      GT518.C67 2008
      391—dc22   2007042756

Chelsea Clubhouse books are available at special discounts when purchased in bulk quantities for businesses, associations, institutions, or sales promotions. Please call our Special Sales Department in New York at (212) 967-8800 or (800) 322-8755.

You can find Chelsea Clubhouse on the World Wide Web at: http://www.chelseahouse.com

Printed and bound in Hong Kong

10 9 8 7 6 5 4 3 2 1

The publishers would like to thank the following for permission to reproduce their pictures:
Corbis: 9 (Wolfgang Kaehler), 12 (Bill Gentile), 19 (Ahmed Jadallah/Reuters), 25 (Jacques Langevin/Sygma).
Mr. Khaled Almaeena/Arab News: 17, 24, 28.
Rex Features: 5 (Sipa Press), 11 and title page, 14 (David Lomax), 20 (K. Nomachi), 21 (Sipa Press), 22 (David Levenson), 23 (Sipa Press), 27 (Hassan Ammar).
Topfoto: 4 (John Moore/Image Works), 6 (Anthony Howarth), 7, 8 (Fratelli Alinari Museum of the History of Photography), 10, 13 (Roger Viollet), 15 (Anthony Howarth), 16 (Anthony Howarth), 18 (AP), 26, 29 (Richard Harding/World Illustrated/Photoshot).

Contents

Saudi Arabia and Its Costume

Saudi Arabia is an enormous country about the size of Western Europe. It occupies about four-fifths of the Arabian Peninsula. The Kingdom of Saudi Arabia was formed in 1932, and Abd al-Aziz al-Saud became its first king. Just a few years later, in 1938, oil was discovered in vast quantities.

A Saudi family on a day trip near the capital, Riyadh. Saudi Arabia used to be a rural society, but now more than four-fifths of the population live in cities.

Saudi Arabia began to sell oil to other countries and rapidly became wealthy. Some of the riches were used to turn the country into a modern state. Roads, schools, hospitals, and housing were built. The towns of Riyadh, Jeddah, Makkah, Madinah, and Dammam mushroomed into major cities with modern facilities.

The Saudi people

Nine out of 10 Saudis are Arabs, including Bedouin Arabs. The Bedouin used to be nomads. They traveled around with their herds looking for good grazing grounds and slept in tents in the desert. Now most Bedouin have settled in towns.

A Muslim country

Saudi Arabia is a Muslim country. Islam is not just a religion, but also a way of life in the kingdom. Five times a day, all activities stop while everyone performs prayers. There are special rules for how men and women should behave and dress. Islamic law states that people should dress modestly. This is taken very seriously in Saudi Arabia.

The Saudi dress code

Both men and women cover their head to go outdoors. Women always wear clothes that cover their arms and legs, and necklines are never low. When they go out, women have to wear an *abaya*, a long, black cloak. To shield the head and face, they put on a cotton or silk headdress called a *tarha*.

On the streets of Saudi Arabia, everyone dresses modestly. Men do not wear shorts in public.

Geography and Climate

Most of Saudi Arabia is desert. During the day, it is baking hot. Temperatures can reach over 122 °F (50 °C) in the summer months. At night, the temperature drops and it feels cool. In the summer, there are strong winds, whipping the desert sand into sandstorms.

This man in the Empty Quarter, the vast desert in the south of the country, wears long, loose clothing. It protects him from the burning sun.

Saudi Arabia has little rainfall—less than 8 inches (200 mm) a year—and there are no rivers. In the west, along the Red Sea coast, there are mountains. Here the climate is cooler, and it sometimes snows in winter.

Desert attire

Loose, long clothes are suited to the desert climate. The Bedouin, traditional desert dwellers, have always worn loose-fitting layers of light-colored clothing. The layers of fabric folded around the body trap air and moisture and keep the body from overheating. Light colors reflect the heat of the sun and keep the wearer cool.

These Bedouin in central Saudi Arabia have stopped by a well to collect water. Their heads are covered for protection.

In the desert, the Bedouin cover their head to protect it from the sun. They draw their head covering around the face to prevent sand from going into their eyes and shade them from the glare of the sun. To cover up in the cool desert evenings, both men and women wear a cloak, called an *abaya* for women and a *bisht* for men. Traditionally, the Bedouin used sheep's wool, camel hair, and goat hair from their herds to make their cloaks.

In the cities, heat does not affect clothing as much. Homes, workplaces, and cars are all air-conditioned.

Cut for the climate

The basic traditional garment is the *thawb*, a body shirt. It varies in different areas according to the climate. In the Najd, the hot central region, Bedouin women wear a very large *thawb* with enormous wide sleeves. The deep folds trap body moisture, while the sleeves catch the breeze. In the cooler highlands of southwestern Saudi Arabia, women wear closer-fitting dresses.

The History of Costume

Traditional Arab costume worn in Saudi Arabia has changed little since ancient times. In the seventh century, the religion of Islam was born in Arabia. The Muslims taught that people should dress modestly. Most people wore long, loose clothing anyway, so their costume changed little.

The basic clothing was similar for men and women. In ancient Arabia, people wore a loincloth as their undergarment. After the Muslims conquered Persia (modern-day Iran) in the mid-seventh century, Arabs adopted the Persian undergarment, called *sirwal*. These thin, loose shorts or pants of varying lengths were cool and comfortable.

Head cloths and cloaks

According to Arabian custom, both men and women covered their head with a head cloth and threw a loose cloak over their *thawb* when they went outdoors. In early Islamic times,

Traditional clothing is similar throughout the Arab world. This is the Algerian Muslim leader Abdelkader, who founded the North African state of Algeria in the 19th century.

8

some cloaks were designed differently for men and women, but often they were similar for both sexes. One old Arabian wrap for men was striped liked a tiger. It was called a *namira* after *nimr*, the Arabic word for "tiger."

Costume changed in some ways during the 20th century. Clothing began to be made in factories, using synthetic as well as natural fibers. Machine stitching replaced traditional embroidery. There used to be important regional differences in dress, but now styles are more uniform.

Regional differences

The traditional dresses of Bedouin women were decorated with colorful embroidery, appliqué, silver, shells, beads, and mother-of-pearl. The decorations varied according to region. In eastern Arabia, the outer edges of the body shirt were embroidered with gold metal thread. On the west coast, tiny beads were sewn onto the garment.

Here you can see the intricate beadwork on a Bedouin woman's dress close-up.

Religion and Culture

When Saudis go outside, they wear special clothes in accordance with the form of Islam practiced in Saudi Arabia. Men cover their head and much of the body, while women cover their head, body, and often their face. Non-Muslim women workers or visitors do not have to cover their face.

Covering up

At a young age, girls cover their head in public with a scarf or bonnet. When they are about nine, they start wearing a head covering that completely hides the hair. It is a common Muslim belief that a woman's hair is part of her beauty, and men outside her family should not see it. All women wear an *abaya* and *tarha* to cover the body and head when they go out. Women who are especially religious also wear a *niqab*, a thick

This Saudi woman wears a black *abaya* and a *niqab* when she goes out. This *niqab* has holes for the eyes.

cotton veil that covers the whole face. It has holes for the eyes or a thin cotton layer at eye level so the wearer can see out.

Keeping cool-headed

Men also cover their head in public, with a *ghutra*. This is a large square piece of white cloth, secured with a doubled black cord called an *igal*. Some men wear a *shumagh*, which is the same as the *ghutra* but has red and white checks. Under the *ghutra*, they wear a small white cotton cap called a *taqiyah*, which helps keep the *ghutra* from slipping off the head.

Women's freedom

The traditional Saudi view is that women should cover up outdoors for their own protection. Men will respect them if they do not show off their bodies. Yet many people outside Saudi Arabia—and some Saudis— feel that women should be free to wear what they want.

These Saudi men are wearing the *shumagh*, secured with an *igal*.

Materials and Textiles

Throughout most of history, the people of Arabia were nomadic, keeping animals and moving around with their herds. (Only about 10 percent of the population is still nomadic today.) The Arabian people used animal fibers from their herds—sheep's wool and goat and camel hair—to make their clothing.

Simple, traditional leather sandals, like some of the pairs left outside this mosque, are called *na'l*.

Traditionally, the best-quality *bishts* were made from camel hair, while the everyday ones were made from sheep's wool. People used cow or camel hide to make leather sandals. From tightly woven black goat

hair and sheep's wool, they formed the *igal*, the black cord that secures a man's headdress.

Modern clothing

Cotton has traditionally been grown in Arabia in small quantities and used for making *thawbs*. These days, most people in Saudi Arabia buy cheap imported clothing produced in factories in Southeast Asia and the Far East. Most *thawbs* are made of cotton, although high-quality women's robes are produced from silk. Lightweight wool is also popular. Saudis prefer clothes made from natural fibers to clothes made of synthetic materials such as polyester and nylon blends because they are cooler in the heat.

Clothing today includes various materials to make pockets, cuffs, zippers, and other fasteners. Decorative features using metal thread, sequins, braids, and embroidery are still popular but are usually machine-made from cheap, synthetic materials.

These men wear typical white cotton *thawbs*.

Traditional dyes

A huge variety of colors used to be produced from all kinds of natural materials, including henna, fermented lemons, and onion skins. The Bedouin in the northwest made bright red dye by boiling white toadstools with alum (a chemical found naturally in some minerals) in the urine of camels.

Men's Clothing

Saudi men still prefer to wear traditional clothes in public and for work, although younger men are starting to buy Western-style clothing.

The basic men's outer garment is the *thawb*. It is a long-sleeved, ankle-length robe with buttons from the neck to the waist. Men wear different varieties depending on the weather. In the summer, they usually wear white or light brown *thawbs* in lightweight cotton. *Thawbs* in darker colors, made from heavier cotton or lightweight wool, are worn in winter.

Men's clothing tends to be plain, without elaborate decoration. Saudis follow the Islamic law that forbids men to wear gold jewelry or silk.

It is normal in Saudi Arabia for men to wear the traditional *thawb* every day.

Cloaks and jackets

Traditionally, men wore a *bisht*, a long cloak, over their *thawb* when they went out. These days, they are more likely to wear a Western-style jacket over their robe. Yet older and wealthier men still wear the *bisht* in public. Most men wear one when they dress up for special occasions. Made from camel hair or wool, the *bisht* usually comes in cream, brown, or black. The most expensive versions have gold braiding on the edges.

In mountainous areas, it is traditional to wear a *farwa*, a jacket made from a single sheepskin. The modern version is a long coat lined with thick sheepskin. Today many men buy imported versions with fake fur linings.

Cool underwear

Saudi men still wear *sirwal* as their undergarment. These loose, comfortable pants are made from cotton or polyester, and some are embroidered at the bottom. Most Saudi men wear short *sirwal*, while those in the western region wear long ones.

Men often pair the *thawb* with a Western-style jacket. But Saudi men do not usually wear a full Western business suit.

Women's Clothing

These days, most women dress in traditional clothes only for special occasions. Traditional dress is the floor-length *thawb*. It comes in different colors, beautifully decorated with brightly colored embroidery and appliqué.

Underneath, women wear a plain shift and underwear similar to men's. On top, villagers (but not city dwellers) may wear a *niqab* and headdress patterned with all kinds of materials, from beads and buttons to coins, shells, and tassels.

At home
Saudi women have been more eager than men to adopt Western clothing. At home and with their female friends and relatives, they relax in

This teacher can loosen her head scarf because she works only with girls.

jeans, tops, and high heels. They often mix traditional fabrics and designs with Western items such as jeans.

At home, girls may wear Western fashions just like European or American children, including sleeveless tops and knee-length skirts. They dress more conservatively to go out.

Out and about

To go out, women dress modestly, always wearing long sleeves and long pants or skirts. Necklines are never low. The black *abaya* that women wear over their clothes in public does not have to be plain. The fabric varies from ordinary cotton to fine silk. Modern Saudi women wear highly decorated *abayas* with embroidery, beading, sequins, ribbons, or lace.

Rania al-Baz was a well-known TV announcer in Saudi Arabia who appeared on the popular program *The Kingdom This Morning*.

Clothes shopping

Saudi men and women are not allowed to work together in any workplace except for hospitals. The store assistants in many women's clothing stores are all men—even in the departments selling ladies' underwear and makeup. All the assistants are male and they cannot staff fitting rooms for female customers. So women have to try on clothes in the ladies' restroom or buy them to try on at home.

Ceremonial and Prayer Costumes

Muslims pray five times a day. At prayer times in Saudi Arabia, businesses close, stores stop selling, and children leave their studies. People can pray wherever they are, placing a prayer mat on the floor facing Mecca.

This boy reads the Koran in his white *thawb* and head covering.

Prayer outfits

Men pray in their white *thawb* and *taqiyah*. Women may wear a robe with a hood. It does not have to be black, so they can choose from a variety of colors. The robe may be patterned too. A woman can throw the robe over whatever she is wearing that day so she can prepare quickly for prayer.

Wedding clothes

For his special day, the groom dresses in white with a *bisht* over the top. The bride also dresses in white. There are separate wedding

parties for men and women, and children can wander between the two. At the female party, women take off their *abaya*, let down their long hair, and dance freely.

At this male wedding party, the men dance together in traditional costume.

Festival dress

There are two major festivals in Islam. Id ul-Fitr is a joyful festival that marks the end of the Ramadan, the month of fasting. It is traditional to buy a new, stylish outfit for the celebrations. Id ul-Adha is the biggest festival, when Muslims remember how Allah tested the faith of the Prophet Ibrahim (Abraham). Again people dress in their best clothes for the huge Id feast.

Henna tattoos

Henna tattoos are popular in Saudi Arabia for weddings and other religious festivals. A few nights before the wedding, the bride and her friends gather for her henna night. The henna artist paints patterns such as flowers, shapes, and spirals on the bride's hands and feet. When it dries, the henna turns a reddish brown color.

Clothing for the Hajj

Every year, around two million pilgrims come to Saudi Arabia for the hajj, the pilgrimage to the holy Islamic sites in and around Mecca.

A pilgrim wears *ihram* on his way to Mecca. Wearing white is a symbol of purity.

It is a duty for all Muslims to make the hajj at least once in their lifetime. The aim of the pilgrimage is to stop all normal activities for a few days and to focus on Allah alone. Many Saudis join the hajj.

Ihram

To help them switch to holy activities, all pilgrims change their clothes. Male pilgrims bathe, shave, and cut their nails. Then they put on a special costume called *ihram*. It is made from simple white garments, which are draped over the body. No sewn clothes are worn. Everyone wears the same clothes to show that all people are equal before God.

A male pilgrim drapes a white sheet around his waist to cover the body from the navel to the ankles. With a strip of *ihram* material, he makes a belt to secure the sheet. He drapes a second sheet over his back and shoulders or just over one shoulder. On his feet, he wears simple sandals that do not cover the toes or heels. He wears neither underwear nor a head covering.

Women can wear modest dress of any color, although they tend to wear ankle-length, long-sleeved white robes. They cover their head but not their hands or face. Dressed in *ihram*, the pilgrims are in a pure state, ready for worship.

Hajj rules

Since everyone is thinking only pure thoughts during the pilgrimage, women do not need to protect themselves by covering their face. So that everyone really does appear the same, no one wears any accessories during the hajj. Men must not wear any jewelry. The only accessory allowed is an umbrella to protect men's bare heads from the fierce sun.

Even women who normally cover their face in daily life do not do so during the hajj.

Work Clothing and Uniforms

Saudi men in many jobs, such as teachers and doctors, wear the traditional *thawb*. Specialists, such as hospital surgeons, wear the same uniform as specialists in other countries.

In the shopping malls, store assistants dress in black pants and white, long-sleeved shirts. Security staff usually wear green pants, white shirts, and green caps.

Police and military uniforms

Military and police uniforms are based on U.S. and British styles because Saudi Arabia modeled its forces on theirs. Soldiers in the army wear khaki uniforms,

These Saudi royal guards, part of the Saudi Arabian army, wear the traditional white *thawb*.

The National Guard

The Saudi Arabian National Guard is the king's private army, with special responsibility for protecting the royal family, the House of Saud, as well as the country in general. National Guardsmen wear the traditional white *thawb* and *ghutra*, which is why the National Guard is also known as the White Army.

while in the navy, blue or white is worn. The air force color is blue. Both military and police personnel wear berets.

Women's clothing

Only a few women work outside the home, although the number is growing. They are expected to dress modestly at work as elsewhere. Village women do not normally cover their face because the *niqab* gets in the way when they are doing manual work. They cover up to go into town, however.

School uniform

Girls and boys are taught separately in single-sex schools. Boys wear a white *thawb* and often a *ghutra*. Girls wear a long dress with a white shirt underneath. The dress colors vary from school to school and for different age groups. In Jeddah, for example, girls wear pink in elementary school and yellow in secondary school. Girls cover up with an *abaya* on the way to school. Inside school, they can remove their *abaya* because all the teachers are female.

Schoolboys walk to school with their mothers. Some of the boys wear a *ghutra*.

Leisure Clothing

Western-style casual clothing is becoming more common in Saudi Arabia, although modest styles are always worn outside the house.

Members of the Saudi soccer team pose in their uniform. The Saudi team is one of the most successful in Asia.

Sports are a popular leisure activity. Saudis enjoy traditional sports, such as falconry and horse and camel racing. The participants usually wear the *thawb* and *ghutra*. Modern sports are on the rise, including soccer, volleyball, basketball, tennis, martial arts, and jogging.

Men jog in T-shirts and sweat suits, while women run in their *abaya*. Women can go swimming at female-only sessions in Islamic uniform— long shorts like bicycle shorts and a long, close-fitting top.

Dance and music

Saudi Arabia has a tradition of folk dance and music, performed at festivals and special events. The national dance is the *ardha*, a sword dance involving singers, dancers, and a poetry narrator. The performers wear regional costumes. In Taif, for example, they wear long, multicolored *thawbs*.

Female groups perform at all-female events such as wedding parties. They dance the *khaliji*, a popular folk dance in the Gulf States. For this, they wear a *thawb nashal*, a long, wide, flowing gown with vast sleeves. Made in a bright color from a semitransparent fabric such as silk, the *thawb* is decorated with metal thread, silk embroidery, beads, and sequins.

Ladies only

There are no movie theaters or bars in the kingdom, and women can take part in few sports. So shopping at the mall is a very popular pastime for women. At the Ladies Kingdom at the Kingdom Center in Riyadh, only women may enter. The staff are entirely female. Women can check in their *abayas* and shop bare-headed in jeans and T-shirts. There are growing numbers of women-only shopping malls in Saudi Arabia.

Women look at the clothes in a store in Dhahran. The fashions they see can be worn at women-only gatherings.

Extras and Accessories

Saudi women love their jewelry. Traditionally, when a woman married, her dowry (money or goods given to the bride by the groom) was offered in jewelry. Saudi brides still receive gifts of jewelry today.

There is a huge selection of gold jewelry on sale at the gold market in Riyadh.

Jewelry

Traditional materials, such as silver, turquoise, gold, pearls, and coins, are commonly used in jewelry. These days, women prefer gold to silver, and jewelry is lighter than it used to be. Islamic designs, such as the "sign of the hand," are popular. In this design, the five fingers stand for the five pillars of Islam—the duties of each Muslim. For this reason, bracelets or rings are often worn in multiples of five. Ear and nose piercing are traditional and still done in rural areas. Many kinds of earrings and nose jewelry can be found in the kingdom.

Cosmetics

Henna and kohl are the only traditional cosmetics. Henna is used to dye the hair and to decorate the skin for special occasions. Kohl is a black eyeliner. Today modern makeup is also available.

Magical jewelry

According to tradition, jewelry has magical powers. For example, turquoise is a popular material because it is believed to ward off the "evil eye." Children are often given silver bracelets or anklets with silver bells. It is thought that the sound of the bells will warn away evil spirits. The bells also amuse small children when they are bored!

Men's accessories

Traditionally, men wore a belt over the *thawb*. The belt is still worn in mountainous and rural areas but not in the cities. The *thawb* may have elaborately decorated cuff buttons to close the cuffs. Men wear no jewelry apart from a watch and a wedding ring.

These men from a village near the city of Jizan, southwest Saudi Arabia, wear a traditional belt with a ceremonial sword.

International Influences

In most Arab countries, people have moved toward adopting Western dress. Saudis have generally stayed with traditional costume, although many women and some men have started to wear Western-style clothes at least part of the time.

Saudi fashion

Saudi Arabia has a growing fashion industry. Its designers are starting to reach an international market. For example, Amina al-Jassim designs a mixture of traditional and high-quality fashionable clothes for Saudi and Muslim women to wear to women-only parties and functions.

Saudi fashion designer Amina al-Jassim (on the right) with other women modeling some of her clothes.

Islamic dress around the world

Islamic dress has had an international influence too. Clothing similar to the Saudi style is worn by women in countries that have adopted Islam as the national religion. Iran's Islamic government has strict laws about costume. When women go out in Iran, they have to wear a long coat over their clothes and cover their heads. In Afghanistan, where a strict dress code was imposed in the mid-1990s, most women still wear a *burqa*, a blue robe that covers the entire body. A small net over the eyes allows the wearer to see.

In many non-Muslim countries in the West, the number of Muslims is increasing—both through immigration and through conversion. As a result more people are wearing Islamic dress. On the streets of Europe, the United States, and Australia, young women wear the head scarf, and a small number even wear a *niqab* or *burqa*.

Abayas with a splash of color

Abayas are now appearing in Saudi malls with colored, beaded drawings on the back. Some have linings in bright colors, flowery patterns, or even leopard skin prints. They are slightly tighter around the middle, giving an idea of the wearer's figure, and do not fasten all the way to the ground. This is a bold move in Saudi Arabia.

Muslim women shop in Paris. The woman at the back wears an *abaya* in Burberry check.

Glossary

abaya A long cloak, normally black, that Saudi women wear over their clothes when they go out. It covers the whole body from the shoulders down.

appliqué A cutout decoration that is fastened to a larger piece of material.

Bedouin *Bedouin* means "desert dweller." It refers to the Arab nomads, who move around with their herds. Most Bedouin these days are settled.

bisht A long cloak worn by men.

burqa A loose garment worn by some Muslim women that covers the face and the entire body down to the ground.

falconry The sport of hunting with falcons, a bird of prey.

farwa Meaning "fur," it refers to a jacket made from a single sheepskin.

ghutra A Saudi man's head covering, made from a square piece of white cloth.

Gulf States The countries around the Persian Gulf: Iran, Iraq, Kuwait, Saudi Arabia, Bahrain, Qatar, the United Arab Emirates, and Oman.

hajj The pilgrimage to Mecca in Saudi Arabia that Muslims are expected to make at least once in their lifetime.

henna A dye made from the leaves of the henna plant. It is used by Saudi women to make patterns on a bride's hands and feet before her wedding.

igal A doubled black cord that men wear around the head to keep the *ghutra* in place.

ihram The simple garments that pilgrims wear, usually made from sheets of white cotton.

Islam The religious faith of Muslims, which includes the belief in Allah as one God and in Muhammad as his final prophet.

khaliji A popular folk dance in Saudi Arabia performed at parties and special celebrations.

kohl A black powder used around the eyes as makeup.

loincloth A single piece of cloth wrapped around the hips.

Mecca This city in western Saudi Arabia is the holiest city in Islam. It is toward Mecca that Muslims turn five times a day in prayer.

na'l Traditional leather sandals worn by men and women that leave the toes and heels uncovered.

namira An old Arabian striped wrap for men, named after *nimr*, the Arabic word for "tiger."

niqab A face veil worn by many women in Saudi Arabia to cover the whole face. It may have holes for the eyes or a thin cotton layer at eye level so the wearer can see out.

nomads People who move from place to place in search of grazing land for their herds.

shumagh A head covering for men. It is the same as the *ghutra* but made from red-and-white-checked material.

sirwal Loose white pants, drawn in at the waist, worn by most Saudi men as underwear. The *sirwal* can either be long or short.

taqiyah A small white hat that men wear directly on the head, under the *ghutra*.

tarha A garment that women use to cover the head when they go out. It is usually made from cotton or fine silk.

thawb The full-length, long-sleeved body shirt, usually white, worn by Saudi men. The *thawb* is also the traditional women's dress and comes in different colors and patterns.

thawb nashal A long, wide flowing dress worn by Saudi women for parties. It is made from a luxury fabric such as silk and decorated with silk embroidery and sequins.

Further Information

Books

Deady, Kathleen W. *Q & A: Saudi Arabia*. Capstone Press, 2005.

Goodwin, William. *Modern Nations of the World: Saudi Arabia*. Lucent Books, 2000.

Senker, Cath. *Countries in the News: Saudi Arabia*. Smart Apple Media, 2007.

Senker, Cath. *Letters from Around the World: Saudi Arabia*. Cherrytree Books, 2007.

Sinkler, Adrian. *The World's Hot Spots—Saudi Arabia*. Greenhaven Press, 2003.

Web sites

www.aminaaljassim.com/
The Web site of Saudi fashion designer Amina al-Jassim.

www.exploresaudiarabia.com/
An educational Web site containing information about Saudi people, places, customs, and culture.

www.saudiaramcoworld.com/index/Subjects.aspx
The Web site of an online magazine called *Saudi Aramco World*. Look for articles under Clothing, Fashion, and Jewelry.

Index